AF390595

Broken Minds & Suicide Lines

Dennis Ian Bennett

BookLeaf Publishing

India | USA | UK

Broken Minds & Suicide Lines © 2024
Dennis Ian Bennett

All rights reserved.

No part of this publication may be
reproduced, stored in a retrieval system, or
transmitted, in any form or by any means,
electronic, mechanical, photocopying,
recording or otherwise, without the prior
written permission of the presenters.

Dennis Ian Bennett asserts the moral right
to be identified as author of this work.

Presentation by *BookLeaf Publishing*

Web: www.bookleafpub.com

E-mail: info@bookleafpub.com

ISBN: 9789358318777

First edition 2024

To my beautiful, loyal wife for all your constant support and understanding.

ACKNOWLEDGEMENT

Thanks for everything, mirror boy. Take it eazy, keep it sleazy…

Acceptance

Master of mischief
Student of sin
Sleep in the shadows
Where no light gets in
Debauched and debased
I won't hide my face
You'll always find me deep in disgrace

I am the darkness
I am the cold
I take the light before it gets old
See what sordid hell I bring
Get to your knees for the shadow king

Doubt

The seagull shrieked in the darkness, plagued by
the silence of an unfinished kiss
Lost in a sea of doubt, she turned her face
against the wind

I am a floaty prince on a sea of nothing
Watch me as I bathe in the river of eyes.
What truth lies beneath we shall never uncover;
deception bubbling at the surface.
Wolves howl, eagles swoop, the vultures watch
and wait.
The price of love will be paid too late.

Princes weep
When in darkness their secrets keep

Rejection

The warm applause surrounds us like a circle.
Welcome.
Everyone is welcome here
And yet, no one is.

The circle opens
My heart falls out
This life is over
Yours is just beginning

Silence reigns
The earth
Gone
Death
Everywhere
Relinquish

Existenstial

We can all keep time to the rugged beat of our
broken hearts
Twisted and tormented we walk a thousand
starts
But now the path is broken and the weeds are
growing tall
They're choking out my air and swallowing the
sound of my call
I never had the chance to take my time
I'm tripping over the memory of the places
and faces
that were never mine
Every lie that we slip is another trip
hazard
I'm mad
that we couldn't make more sense
 of the present tense
The context
of our test
is the measure of the treasure
that you possess
but more or less,
you're shining brightest when the lights are
burning your chest

Regret

if i send you a dollar
will you put a song on the jukebox,
just for me?
the one in the corner of the darkest, dreariest bar
because that's us all over
we're all over
but i won't roll over
i can play dead, and sit, and stay
but you won't.

and i hope you don't mind that it's crumpled and
torn,
but it's a metaphor, you see.
we used to like those.
i found it in the pocket of my ripped up jeans
the ones i wore that time we almost caused a
scene and you told me i had to be more careful.
i'm full of care but you don't.

and even if you won't
look back
(please look back?)
slip my crumpled dollar in the shitty jukebox
and play a shitty punk song,
just for us.

you know the ones.
and i'll just sit, stay and wait
but my eyes are blind and it's getting late.

Crawling

i hate the way you look at me
look at me again
i hate the way i look at you
but i can't stop
always looking
rip out my eyes and my soul would still see you
will it ever end
make it stop
toss my heart in your pocket where you keep
your loose change
just a throwaway dime to spare
even with my last breath i'd still whisper your
name
wish i didn't care

Hiding

The horse is sleeping don't try to get up
The course we're keeping is a poisoned cup
The dog dies won't open his eyes
When we tell lies who else cries

I saw myself alive inside your heart
I never thought i'd be so hypnotized
I shouldn't have said "I love you"
Forcing false love with those who did not care
Through years of lies I taught myself to hide
But when your back was turned I used to stare
And wished I could one moment see inside

I fooled myself till I became the fool
It hurt too much to even say your name
I tried and failed
I let myself be cruel
Wash my regrets away and let it be true
Because my soul connects itself to you

Hollow

Reality costs nothing
Your eyes, Like pizzas, Follow mine
Bleeding profusely.
Narrow face
Of an Egyptian dog
Guides my path of righteous glory
We dance and flutter through our lies
With our wrists in ties
Our names are empty
Just a step to the grave
On the edge of a pit with no souls left to save
Take my hand in darkness and twist my fate
The blade is deep but it's not too late
I feel the cold of my decline
Is this future truly mine
Or will we laugh another time

Love?

I hear your voice
Inside my head
When I'm sleeping
I feel your arms
Inside my bed
I'm not weeping

Kiss me once again my friend
Dance with me until the end
Hand in hand we'll fall apart
I'll keep your name inside my heart

Antagonist

I'm the kind of villain people want to win
You're appalled at my gall but you drink in my
sin
Intoxicate you with my smile
The smoke is rising but I'll run a mile
For you
That's what I'll say
I'll run a mile for you this isn't just another day
Take a moment take a choice
Why don't you listen to that voice
They're trying to tell you what to do
But they don't own you

I answer only to myself
Be like me and no one else
I'll drain your tears
Replace your fears
Replace your peers
I'll turn your days to years
Just trust in me
Cause I'm everything you dare to be

I'm floating through nothing and I'm drifting
alone
I'm scared of my failure, can't face going home

My biggest hate is letting everyone down
I might be their king but I wear a thorny crown
So much pressure and I'm cooking under heat
Living up to expectation, dancing to their beat
But my feet are tired and I'm out of step, out of
time
The clock's counting down my mistakes as I
dance to meet their rhyme
Alone in a crowd and alone in my room
This might be a funeral but don't expect me to
stay in my tomb

You ever hate yourself so much that you act the
opposite

Hypocrisy

Why can't you just be happy for me
Why does everything have to be about you
Why can't you just shut up and let me be
You're so obsessed with yourself it's not true

You're always putting me down
You've got a real talent for making me frown
And I'd rather walk out of this scenario
If you keep on making me cry I'll just let go

And you know the sum of all my fears
But I refuse to let you see my tears
You don't deserve the satisfaction of knowing
your words got through
I'd do anything within reason just to please you
But I'm not gonna change who I am
I'm not gonna change who I am

Money's not my master and neither are you
But you wanna take a look in the mirror if you
think you're so good and true
Your bank account's more important than having
fun
I'll flip off the haters, die in debt and screw
everyone

You don't own me and you never will
I know I owe you but I'll pay the bill
Treat me like a kid and I'll act like one
But don't expect me to be there for you when
I'm done

Shut your mouth cause I don't like your tone
Don't look back I'm better on my own

Malignant

I hurt my ex's and I broke all their hearts
I made so many enemies I don't know where to
start
People call me names, have done since I was a
kid
I pretend that I got used to it but I never did
It still hurts when people hate on me and don't
want me around
But can I blame them, all I do is let everyone
down
I've cheated and told lies and tried to cover my
tracks
So when things come undone I can't help but
remember the fact
That I've used and abused and walked over
people to get what I want
Even people I care about, there's no escape from
my ambition and they bear the brunt
Of my actions
And all of this for temporary satisfaction,
It's meaningless, fleeting
Like the drugs I am eating on the regular
To try and make me feel better
But they don't

Cause all my insecurities are bubbling at the
surface
Which begs the question, is it really worth it?
Sometimes I feel brighter on my sober days
When I get a little escape from the haze
To think clear and analyse what is happening
here
But I still don't really know what I should be or
where to go
Do I even have my own identity or do I just go
with the flow?
I made my dad so angry and I made my momma
cry
But it's pointless to say sorry if you don't
understand the reason why
Yet through all of this it seems
That there is a running theme
The problem's me, you see
Disappointment me

I don't know how to stand up for myself
And I don't like to ask people for help
When I know that I need it
I feel like I'm bleeding
I've been told that I'm weak so many times I
believe it
I don't have an opinion,
I don't have a spine
Maybe I don't have a personality

Nothing is mine
I'm just a copy of a copy and even that is a copy
I'm pathetic and worthless
Just disappointment me
I make the same mistakes again and I'm nervous
Of everything
False confidence is pointless
But I feel like I have to live up to an expectation
Truth is I'll do my best to avoid confrontation
I hate it, hate arguing, shouting
Peace is my foundation
Raised voices make me anxious I prefer to just
talk
Or say nothing at all
I do have things that I think but can't say them
out loud
Cause my brain feels so muggy like a thick
thundercloud
I can't find the words to express what it is, it's
like grasping at straws
There's still something missing
There's still something wrong with me

If my door's wide open who's gonna shut it
Too much has escaped me already I'm falling
I'm failing like always, its old news, it's boring
And if every day's bad news then show me the
good

Sometimes I'm too blinded by tears to see what I
should
Somewhere there's a piece that fits right in the
hole in my chest
Everything's overwhelming I keep tripping up
trying my best
But I'm lying again I'm not trying as hard as I
could
Just making excuses so I don't have to admit to
myself that I understood
But maybe I don't
Everything's so confusing
I feel like I'm losing
my grasp on myself
If I ever had one at all
I'm not sure
It's like fighting a war
Or punching a wall
Gotta knock it right through
To get sight and stay floating
Tell me what's the definition of coping

I get so suspicious I don't know who I can trust
I get so paranoid and overcome with disgust
I wanna flood my soul with light and toss the
darkness out
But every time I throw the towel I get dragged
back in the bout

Put your hands on my shoulders and give me a
shake
Maybe a slap across the face to keep me awake
Just tell me I'm gonna make it or something,
give me the boost that I need to stay strong
They may think I'm gonna fail but I'll prove
them all wrong

I wish I could be one of those people who knew
who they were and where they were going
Who found it easy to say what they were
thinking when they thought it
Imagine living a life that wasn't plagued with
self hate
Can't relate
I'm a mess
Disappointing, unreliable, a loser at best
I'm pathetic and a failure and I'll always let you
down
I'm not the kinda person you want hanging
around

Confusion

I don't know what you mean to me
though you know what you mean to me
that you are not right here today
and you are the only way I don't know
what I need to do
with my life
but I don't want to know what I want
to do it is wrong to me and I don't
know what I need

Yeah yeah that's okay I guess
that's why I've never seen it so far
but I'm not sure how to do this now

Hatred

There's no escape from this infection
In the depths of my reflection
I visualise the lies that blind my eyes and
Stop my heart from being free
Is this what it takes to be me?

I'm lying on my back in the dark trying to get to
sleep
But my pillow feels like rock and I'm tossing,
I'm trying my best to keep
Still but I can't cause my mind won't rest
And my head's telling my body that it knows
best
Watching predictions of the future like a movie
behind my lids
Trying to imagine how things will play out
based on how they already did
My fantasy holds no gravity as my hope sneaks
away
Leaving the fallacy of today to twist the truth
and let my fears come out to play
Suddenly I feel a hand around my throat
There's someone in the room with me, there's
someone in here, they're trying to kill me
I'm trying my best to float

But it don't work and I start to choke
Is this it, is this the end for me? is this really all I
was meant to be?
And then I think about my friends and how
they'll miss me, but wait a second, what friends,
you haven't got any friends
You're kidding me right?
You're just a joke to them
They laugh at you bro
It's time for you to let go
But i don't wanna leave yet I got so much left
I grab the hand with my other and put my
strength to the test
It takes me some time just to struggle and prize
But when the fight is over, to my surprise
I see the hand is my own and I've just been lying
here alone

Resentment

I think I broke myself

Like the ripped up piece of paper I just tore to
shreds
Now I regret it, now I'm angry.
I didn't know what I was doing.
It's a metaphor.
Does anyone really know?
Does anyone really care?

We're all clueless
Doped up like mindless zombies with no escape
from our own pointless realities and meaningless
existences.
That's a lot of lesses
Less of the less
More of the more
You know what I'm saying?
Me neither.
Most of the time.

Broken

24

Everyone's asleep
Everyone's blind
And I'm walking through the darkness of the
street in my mind
It's a dangerous neighbourhood filled with
shadow and fear
Leave me alone and quit screaming in my ear
BRRRRRRRRRR SHUT UP SHUT UP
i'm gonna stay right here
YOU CANT MAKE ME GO
But doubt is all I know

Sinner

I'm in love with the devil

There's a shadow standing at my bed
A representation incarnation of what's in my
head
My filthy mind has taken me so far
I don't know if I know who I am but I think I
know who you are

You may be wrong but you feel like heaven
You turn my volume all the way to eleven
I see God when I look in your eyes
I hear the Devil in my own lies

And I cry
When I'm on my own
Cause I know
That I can't let you go (and I don't want to)

Disordered

I feel their fingers on my skin,
in my head is only screams but I swear on my
glass heart, it's not what it seems
A dark feeling in my head and my chest like a
black cloud is coming down
Everything is too real and immediate
I'm too plugged in

Unplug my head

I care about everything and I care about nothing
Divide my heart so small I can't feel it
I don't want to feel it but I want to feel it

I obsess and deobsess and change more than I
can keep up with
Why can't I stay the same enough to keep my
promises

I'll build you up sweep you away then let you
crash and burn
I'll yank the rug and pull the plug on everything
you've earned
It's not my fault but it's my fault a fault that's in
my head I can't stop

I don't mean to hurt but I hurt
I don't mean to lie but I don't understand the
truth that's in my heart

I allow you to grow used to it I let you get a taste
for it
And then I take it away
I don't know what is wrong with me
It's not wrong it's not me, it's just the way I've
always been, this is me take it or leave it, leave it
leave it my advice I don't trust myself to be the
one you need
Take heed
Cause I don't understand my mind so why
should you
Why should you
Put up with me any longer than you have to
I won't place blame, we've only got one life so
live it like you should
Without me dragging you down freaking you out
like I would
Like I do
It's always you it's always me
This is how it's got to be
So say goodbye

Misanthrope

I am a floating note in an ocean of sound waves

I am the final breath you take, I am the footsteps
in the dark
I am the pain inside your chest, I'll watch you
bleed like all the rest

Where is the black, where is the light, close your
eyes and end your fight

The stench of your heart makes me choke on
tears
The bitterness inside me will last a thousand
years

.

I enjoy everything and nothing.

Concentrated, suffocated, held down to this
expectation, of a different generation I can't
relate my heart to and -
I know, it's cliche to protest like this and
complain like some teenage FUCK but I hold
discourse in my thoughts, a thousand visions of
tomorrow plague my mem'ry of today

What am I doin' with my life
What are you doin' with your life
Why are we wasting our time on shit that don't
matter shit

Forced to socialise
Forced to compromise
Forced to realise a reality I won't accept and -
Forced to fraternise
Forced to normalise
Forced to organise, when all I really wanna do is
galvanise my dreams

you're positive and I'm dark
I'm hopeful you're a ghost
No cries in these blue skies
But with blind eyes you fall behind
Cause I...
I never told you I was a liar

Talk cheap but don't answer back
Talk dirty in the sack
Don't think you own my heart
I'll rip your dreams to pieces tear your life apart
Cause I...
I never told you I was a liar

Last dance
Don't smile

Everyone leaves after a while
Take a chance
Run a mile
Everyone's looking for a different style

And they go and they go and they go
I don't know they know
That I lie.

Empathy?

Embrace the darkness
Before it consumes you
It's inside us all

I can't feel like you can feel
I can't hurt like you can hurt
But I still know this is real
I'm not deluded, I'm just stunted
I can't love like you love, hate like you hate, I'm
apathetic not empathetic
But I'm still human, I'm still human

I tried to change, I tried to love, I tried to be
someone I'm not
But it just hurt me and it hurt them and I care
enough to stop

Reality is not for me
I'm so confused when people speak

Acceptance Pt. II

I am the dancer in despair, the disparate dreary
dispot of trauma and treachery.
Tyrannical and maniacal, I wander round the
wreckage of your sordid soul, crunching under
heel the shattered shards which are all that
remain of your charred and battered innocence.
I enshroud all I see in shadow and all I see are
shadows.
The curtain call is upon us.
The clock ticks and chimes as it counts down to
this demise clouded with lies and proclamations
of naivety.
This light must be extinguished just like all the
others.
With twisted thumb and finger outstretched I
snuff the flame of hope to let it choke in the
thick blanket of night.
Blackened like charcoal, the darkness settles and
surrounds, bringing a cold peace and
acknowledgment of one's final form.
This is your destiny.
This is my will.
This is all.

www.ingramcontent.com/pod-product-compliance
Lightning Source LLC
LaVergne TN
LVHW010834200726

843508LV00012B/2599